SIX MILLION PAPER CLIPS

We did what we had to do.
We try to honor the dead
and tell the world that there is
no substitute for tolerance.
Are you listening?
Please come to Whitwell
and see for yourself.

— The Students of
Whitwell Middle School

SIX MILLION PAPER CLIPS

THE MAKING OF A CHILDREN'S HOLOCAUST MEMORIAL

PETER W. SCHROEDER & DAGMAR SCHROEDER-HILDEBRAND

KAR-BEN PUBLISHING • MINNEAPOLIS

The authors would like to thank the children of Whitwell.
We are proud and humbled that they call us their friends, and we thank
all people of good will on both sides of the Atlantic Ocean who made
The Children's Holocaust Memorial *possible and who give us hope.*

Text copyright © 2004 by Peter W. Schroeder and Dagmar Schroeder-Hildebrand

KAR-BEN PUBLISHING, INC.
A division of Lerner Publishing Group
241 First Avenue North
Minneapolis, MN 55401 U.S.A.
1-800-4KARBEN

Website address: www.kar-ben.com

Library of Congress Cataloging-in-Publication Data

Schroeder, Peter W., 1942–
    Six million paper clips : the making of a children's Holocaust memorial / by Peter W. Schroeder and Dagmar Schroeder-Hildebrand.
       p. cm.
    ISBN-13: 978-1-58013-169-8 (lib. bdg. : alk. paper)
    ISBN-10: 1-58013-169-7 (lib. bdg. : alk. paper)
    ISBN-13: 978-1-58013-176-6 (pbk. : alk. paper)
    ISBN-10: 1-58013-176-X (pbk. : alk. paper)
    1. Holocaust, Jewish (1939–1945)—Study and teaching (Elementary)—Tennessee—Whitwell—Juvenile literature.
    2. Holocaust memorials—Tennessee—Whitwell—Juvenile literature. 3. Whitwell (Tenn.)—Ethnic relations—Juvenile literature.
    4. Whitwell Middle School (Whitwell, Tenn.)—Juvenile literature. I. Schroeder-Hildebrand, Dagmar,1943–II. Title.

D804.33.S34 2004
940.53'18'071276879—dc22   2004019598

Manufactured in the United States of America
9 10 11 12 13 14 – DP – 11 10 09 08 07 06

INTRODUCTION

STRANGE THINGS are going on at Whitwell Middle School.

Inside the school, giant paper clips dangle from the ceiling, and the hallways are adorned with cutouts of butterflies. Outside is something that doesn't seem to belong: a small piece of railway track.

Whitwell never had a rail connection to the world. The old coal mine closed years ago, and its rail connection didn't go all the way to the town.

But today, welded to this small piece of track, sits a railcar. It is a small boxcar, not of the sort you normally see in the United States.

The railcar is surrounded by a well-tended garden with flowers, shrubs, and copper sculptures. Next to it stands an eight-foot-high iron cubicle with a big, shiny paper clip and metal statues of a girl and boy catching butterflies.

On one side of the boxcar a sign reads "Holocaust-Mahnmal der Kinder." On the other side, this German inscription is translated: "The Children's Holocaust Memorial."

THIS SEALED, IRON MONUMENT CONTAINS 11 MILLION PAPER CLIPS.

CHAPTER ONE

TEACHING DIVERSITY

WHITWELL, TENNESSEE

WHITWELL, TENNESSEE, is a small town nestled in the Sequatchie Valley, over the mountains from Chattanooga. The middle school is located on Main Street across from a small clapboard-style church. It is a town where everyone knows everyone. Only 1,600 people live in Whitwell.

"We take care of each other," Whitwell Middle School principal Linda Hooper says proudly. "But we are all alike: white, Anglo-Saxon, and Protestant. You can count the minority families on one hand. There are no foreigners in Whitwell—and no Catholics, no Muslims, no Jews."

Mrs. Hooper knows that growing up in a small community where everyone is alike can be a drawback. "One day, our kids will leave the sheltered life in Whitwell. They will work in a big town over the mountains, or go on vacation to visit relatives or friends. And they will encounter people who are not 'like us.' How will they handle intolerance or rejection?"

In the spring of 1998, one parent, who had been a student of Mrs. Hooper's 25 years earlier, suggested that it was time to teach diversity. But how?

Some months later, David Smith, the school's vice principal and coach of the Whitwell Tigers' football team, attended a teachers' conference in Chattanooga. He came back to Whitwell both disturbed and excited.

"Mrs. Hooper," he asked his boss, "what do you know about the Holocaust?"

"You mean the extermination of the Jews by the Nazis?" she replied. "Why do you ask?"

"Because now I know how we can teach diversity," he exclaimed. "We can tell the kids what happened to the Jewish people. We can demonstrate what intolerance is and what it can lead to."

Linda Hooper didn't need any convincing. She started planning what nobody had done at Whitwell Middle School before: to teach a special class about the Holocaust and the roots of intolerance.

In the fall, she summoned the parents of all eighth graders. "The Holocaust class will be a voluntary, after-school project," she explained. "And we will ask all parents to attend the first sessions, because we will talk about disturbing and horrific things."

Nobody said a word. Some parents shuffled uncomfortably on the seats of the little chairs. In this silence, Mrs. Hooper said, "If anyone thinks we shouldn't go ahead, please speak up now."

One father raised his hand. "Linda, would you want your own children to attend the Holocaust class?" he asked.

"I would," she replied. "My kids didn't learn about the Holocaust at school, so I had to teach them at home."

"Then we're all on board," the father said. All the other parents nodded their heads in agreement.

There was no question who should teach the class. Sandra Roberts, the popular eighth-grade language arts teacher, was the natural choice. Sandra had been one of Mrs. Hooper's students.

Sandra herself didn't know much about the Holocaust. For two weeks, she read every related book she could lay her hands on, and she researched the subject on the Internet. "I basically knew what had happened," she would confess much later, "but I didn't realize the enormity of the systematic mass murder of the Jewish people."

At the first class, Sandra introduced the subject of the Holocaust to the 16 students who had enrolled in the class. "Some 70 years ago, the leader of the Nazi Party, Adolf Hitler, became head of the German government. He hated Jews and blamed them for all the ills of the German society. He ordered that they be punished. The punishment began with laws that restricted the rights of Jews. Later the Jews were herded into ghettos, transported to concentration camps, and forced to work as slave laborers.

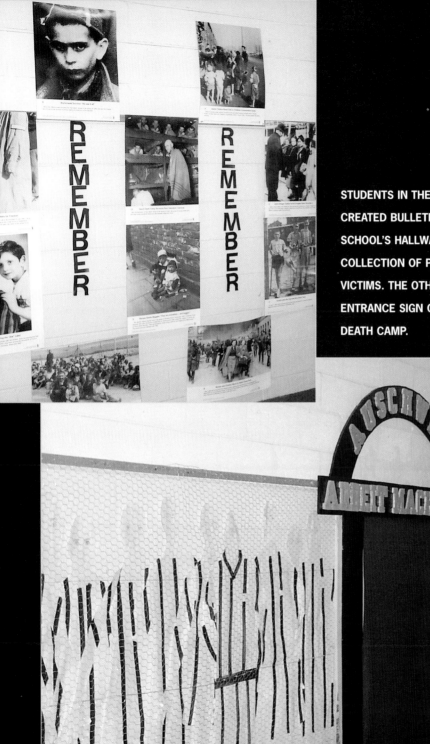

STUDENTS IN THE HOLOCAUST CLASS CREATED BULLETIN BOARDS FOR THE SCHOOL'S HALLWAY. ONE IS A COLLECTION OF PHOTOS OF HOLOCAUST VICTIMS. THE OTHER REPLICATES THE ENTRANCE SIGN OF THE AUSCHWITZ DEATH CAMP.

In the end, the punishment, over and over again, was death."

The students in the Holocaust class looked at their teacher in disbelief. "You are joking," one girl said, "and you shouldn't joke about murder."

In the following weeks, the students discovered that the teacher wasn't joking. They all read *The Diary of Anne Frank*, the journal of a teenage girl who had hidden with her family for over two years in Nazi-occupied Amsterdam. Then they read *I Have Lived a Thousand Years: Growing up in the Holocaust* by Livia Bitton-Jackson, the story of 13-year-old Ellie Friedman, who was forced from her home, along with her family, to the concentration camp of Auschwitz.

Sandra Roberts was concerned how her pupils would react when she told them that the Nazis planned to wipe out the Jewish race completely. "They didn't just murder a few Jews here and there," she told her students. "The Nazis murdered six million Jews. And between one and two million of these victims were children. Children like you."

There was an eerie silence in the classroom. The students looked at their teacher without any emotion. "Didn't they hear what I told them?" she asked herself. She repeated, "The Nazis murdered six million Jews."

Finally, one girl raised her hand. "This sounds awful, really awful, Ms. Roberts, but what on earth is six million?"

"Yeah, how much is it?" echoed a classmate. "I can't imagine a number as large as six million."

"I can't either," Sandra admitted. "Any suggestions?"

"We could collect six million of something and pile it up," one boy proposed.

"Good idea," said someone else. "But what should we collect?"

Everyone had a different idea. Buttons and pennies were suggested. But none seemed realistic.

"What about collecting paper clips?" one student asked. "That shouldn't be too difficult."

"Who gave you that idea?" Sandra asked.

"The Internet, Ms. Roberts," the student answered. "I read on my mom's computer that the paper clip played a big role in the Holocaust. The Nazis invaded the country of Norway, and they began to round up Jews to ship them to concentration camps. The non-Jewish Norwegians didn't like it a bit. And so they protested . . . by wearing paper clips."

STUDENTS CREATED A PYRAMID OF SHOES TO RECALL THE MILLIONS OF SHOES LEFT BEHIND BY THOSE WHO PERISHED IN THE DEATH CAMPS.

Sandra Roberts didn't know what to make of the story. But she had been teaching long enough to know that a teacher often can learn from a student. "Go on," she said. "That can't be the end of the story."

The student continued. "The Nazis forced Jews to wear yellow stars on their clothing. So the Norwegians began to wear paper clips on their lapels as a protest."

Sandra Roberts did her own research. Not only was the story true, but a Norwegian man, Johan Vaaler, had invented the paper clip in 1899.

So the Holocaust class of the Whitwell Middle School began to collect paper clips.

At that moment, nobody could imagine that life would never be the same at Whitwell Middle School . . . or in the little town in the Sequatchie Valley.

CHAPTER TWO

COLLECTING PAPER CLIPS

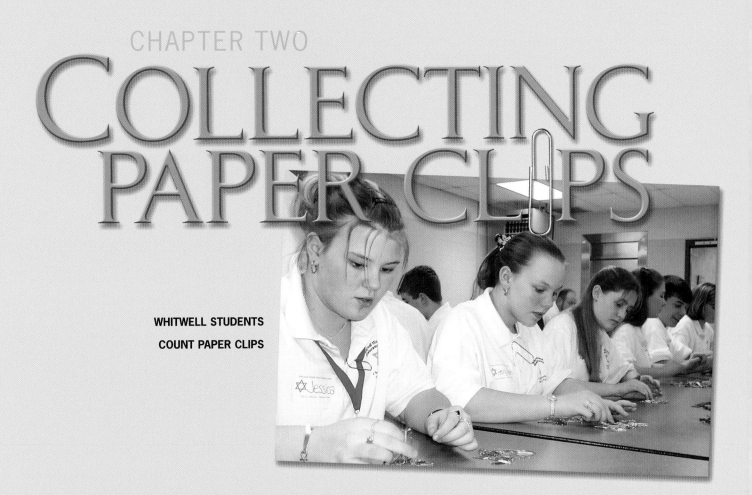

**WHITWELL STUDENTS
COUNT PAPER CLIPS**

THE STUDENTS went through every drawer at home, and they asked relatives and neighbors to do the same. After a few weeks, they had brought more than 1,000 paper clips to school.

They realized that collecting six million was not going to be so easy. So they began writing letters to sports heroes, politicians, film stars, and industry leaders asking for help. Most wrote back and told the students how impressed they were to learn about their project. And they sent paper clips.

While most of the paper clips came from "regular folks," packages also came

15

in from famous people such as former president Bill Clinton, actor Tom Hanks, director Steven Spielberg, and football players from the Tampa Bay Buccaneers and the Dallas Cowboys.

WHITWELL STUDENTS OPEN THE MAIL AND UNPACK BOXES.

With the paper clips came letters, such as one from Hollywood director Henry Winkler whose father was a Holocaust survivor. The star of the TV series *Happy Days* told the students that when his father fled the Nazis and immigrated to the United States, he had to leave everything behind. But he was determined to keep a very old pocket watch he had received as a Bar Mitzvah* gift from his father. He covered it with melted chocolate and smuggled it out in an old box. Winkler received the watch when he became a Bar Mitzvah and has since passed it on to his son.

*Hebrew for "son of the commandment." At age 13, Jewish boys become adults in terms of their obligations and privileges in the eyes of the Jewish community. This milestone is usually celebrated at a synagogue service followed by a party.

The students organized a system to deal with the deluge of mail. Some logged in the letters and put them into binders, while others counted and stored the paper clips. Soon the letters filled nine scrapbooks, and the clips began overflowing their containers.

The students were excited about the mail, but they soon realized that they probably would never reach their goal.

Coach David Smith, who had joined the Holocaust group as an adviser, came up with an idea. He proposed designing a website to explain the Paper Clip Project and ask for contributions. A few days later, the website was up and running. "Please help us," it said. "We are collecting paper clips. Each

ORGANIZING LETTERS OF ENCOURAGEMENT AND PERSONAL ACCOUNTS FROM HOLOCAUST SURVIVORS

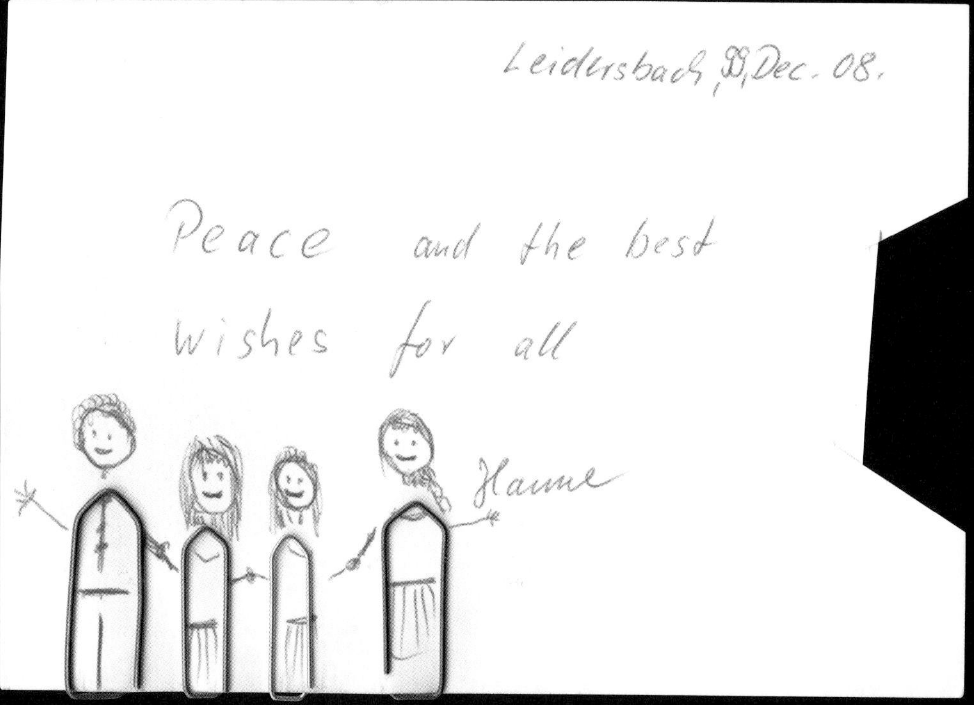

Leidersbach, 29. Dec. 08.

Peace and the best wishes for all

Hanne

A POSTCARD FROM GERMANY

Wassili Loukopoulus-Lepento
Herbstfelder im Odenwald
120×68 1979
Fall fields in Oden Forest
Φθινοπωρινά πεδία στό Odenwald

POPP

KUNSTKARTE

NR 3108 POPP-VERLAG HEIDELBERG

Harald Mechthild Christine Yannick

Es war mir einfach und spontan ein Bedürfnis, mich + meine Familie zu beteiligen
Mechthild (47) Harald (47)
Christine (14) + Yannick (11)
Rupp aus Heidelberg
4 x der Wunsch, dass SOETWAS nie nie wieder passiert. Danke.

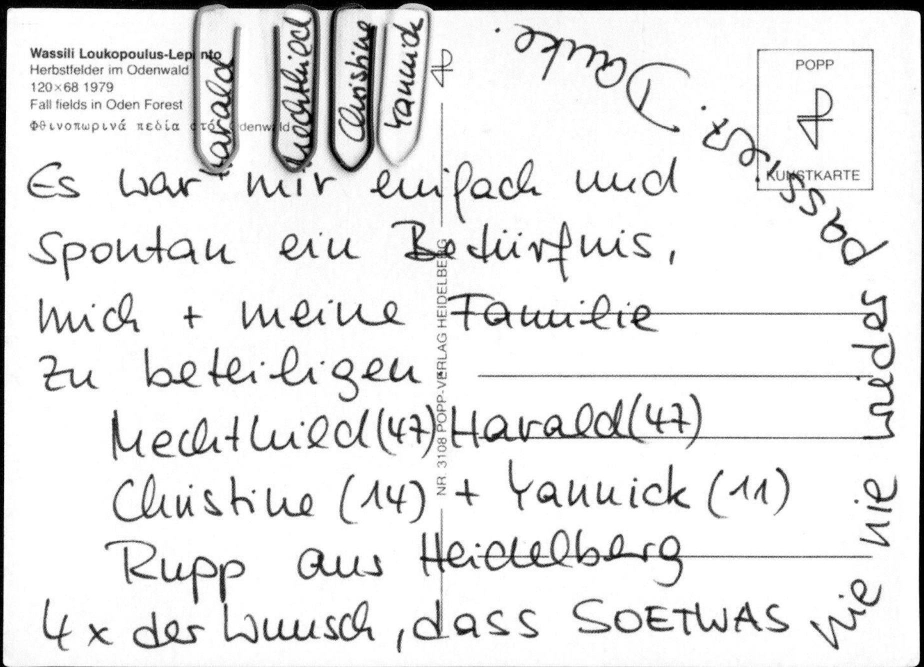

A FAMILY IN GERMANY WRITES: "WE HOPE THAT IT WILL NEVER HAPPEN AGAIN."

one will represent a victim of the Holocaust. As soon as we have six million, we will make a monument."

Hundreds of people responded with letters of encouragement . . . and paper clips.

But after some time, the excitement died down, and at the end of the year, the Holocaust group had received only 160,000 paper clips. The students did the math and found that at this rate, it would take 37.5 years to reach their goal.

"We will never understand what six million victims really means," one student said sadly. The teachers tried to convince the students not to give up hope.

Help for the project was already on the way. But nobody in Whitwell knew it.

CHAPTER THREE
THE LINK TO GERMANY

IN THE FALL OF 1999, Dagmar and Peter Schroeder, White House correspondents for a group of German newspapers, came across the project's website at the U.S. Holocaust Memorial Museum in Washington, D.C. The very same day, they had lunch with their dear friend, 92-year-old Lena Lieba Gitter, who had fled to the United States from her native Austria after the Nazis had taken over that country.

Amazingly, Lena met the Schroeders at the door of her Washington home with a printout of the Whitwell website. And as she served them lunch, she urged them, "Do something about this! I know you will."

PHOTOS OF STUDENTS IN A CLASS IN GERMANY THAT PARTICIPATED IN COLLECTING PAPER CLIPS

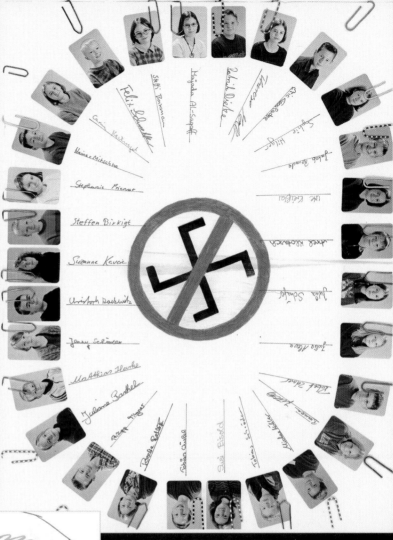

A YOUNG GERMAN BOY'S DRAWING CONNECTING PEOPLE OF THE WORLD WITH PAPER CLIPS

So they did. They called the school and talked to the teachers and some students. They wrote articles for nine German newspapers that included a simple request. "If you think this project is worthwhile, please send some paper clips. And enclose a letter telling the students why you are participating."

In the first three weeks after the articles appeared, the students received 2,000 letters and counted more than 46,000 paper clips. Letters came from children as young as six. The oldest writer was ninety-eight.

Some former German soldiers apologized for "not being heroes" during the war. Survivors wrote and told their stories. The Whitwell students heard from other school classes that had started their own paper clip collections. Over and over people wrote, "We want to do our part, so that history will not be repeated."

The paper clips came in all colors, shapes, and sizes, as different as humans are . . . and as alike. Many letters came with poems, drawings, and other artwork.

The Schroeders received so many deeply touching letters that they decided to write a book about the German response. *Das Büroklammer-Projekt (The Paper Clip Project)* was published in Germany in the fall of 2000.

When *Washington Post* editor Dita Smith read the book, she decided she needed to know more. She traveled to Whitwell, and on April 7, 2001, which coincided with Passover,* she published an article in the *Washington Post* entitled "A Measure of Hope." Other newspapers and TV and radio stations all over the country picked up the story and told their readers, viewers, and listeners what the kids in Whitwell were up to.

"If you want to help—send paper clips," they urged.

---

*A Jewish holiday celebrated in the spring that commemorates the Exodus of the Israelites from Egypt.

CHAPTER FOUR

PLANNING THE MEMORIAL

ONE OF THE BOXES FILLED WITH PAPER CLIPS THAT ARRIVED AT WHITWELL MIDDLE SCHOOL

Aᴺᴅ PEOPLE DID! The post office in Whitwell received so many letters and packages every day that the letter carrier couldn't fit them all in his car. So the postmaster began calling Linda Hooper to send someone to pick up the mail. On some days, Vice Principal Smith had to make several trips to the post office in his pickup truck.

At the school, there were not enough hands to count all the paper clips. So parents came to school and counted. Soon others joined them. On some days, there were more grown-ups in the school than students.

23

TEACHER SANDRA ROBERTS *(AT RIGHT, BEHIND STUDENT)* **AND STUDENTS PLACE PAPER CLIPS IN A STORAGE BARREL.**

In Washington, the Schroeders were also receiving mail and paper clips. They loaded them in their car and drove down to Whitwell. The students greeted them excitedly. "You will not believe this! We have more than five million paper clips! One million more to go!"

"What should we do if we get more than six million?" one student asked.

"Keep on collecting and counting," the Schroeders told them. "The Nazis didn't murder only Jews. They murdered others as well."

Dagmar told the students about a lady she had met while studying at the University of Cologne in Germany. She was 4 feet 1½ inches tall. Had she been only 4 foot 1 inch, she would have been killed, because the Nazis were murdering very short people. They called them *Unwertes Leben* (unworthy life).

The students learned that the Nazis also killed political opponents, Socialists, Communists, handicapped people, Jehovah's Witnesses, homosexuals, and others—everyone who didn't believe in or didn't fit into their ideology of a superior race. There were actually 11 million victims.

"We will not stop," the class agreed. "We will collect 11 million paper clips!"

The paper clips kept coming and coming. Soon the school looked like a warehouse. There were packages and boxes everywhere—in classrooms, in the cafeteria, in the library, in the broom closet, in the principal's office, and under the floor of the gymnasium. They were becoming a fire hazard. The time had come to decide what to do with all the paper clips. The time had come to create a Holocaust memorial at Whitwell Middle School.

One evening, Linda Hooper, her husband Ed, Sandra Roberts, David Smith, his wife Laura, and the Schroeders met for dinner at a local restaurant.

STACKS OF BOXES UNDER THE FLOOR OF THE MIDDLE SCHOOL GYMNASIUM

"We started the project because we wanted to have an idea what six million lives means," Sandra said. "It's not decent to leave all the paper clips lying around. We need a memorial for them."

But what should it look like?

Initially, the students had thought that all the paper clips could be melted down at a local ironworks and made into a big metal sculpture . . . perhaps a stop sign with a paper clip and a swastika, the symbol of the Nazi movement.

But after learning how hundreds of thousands of Jews were burned in crematories, the students knew that melting down the paper clips was out of the question. "Each paper clip represents a murdered victim of the Holocaust," they told Sandra Roberts. "We can't burn them again!"

The adults tried to come up with another idea. They discussed putting all the paper clips in a big glass jar or attaching them to a giant magnet. Sandra Roberts recalled the visit the students had made to the Holocaust Museum in Washington. She remembered the feelings they had had as they walked through a cattle car the Nazis had used to transport prisoners to concentration camps.

"That's it!" Dagmar and Linda exclaimed at the same time. "We need to find an original German railcar to house the paper clips."

The Schroeders were convinced that finding, securing, and shipping a railcar to Whitwell was a done deal. The rest of the evening was spent thinking about designs for the memorial.

But no one knew how difficult the search for an original German railcar would be.

WHILE THE SCHROEDERS SEARCHED
FOR A RAILCAR, PAPER CLIPS AND
LETTERS CONTINUED TO POUR IN
FROM AROUND THE WORLD.

CHAPTER FIVE

SEARCHING FOR A RAILCAR

PETER AND DAGMAR thought there would be hundreds of railcars still
rolling around Germany. The Germans are known for building sturdy things.
What is 60, 70, or even 80 years for a railcar?

"Three days tops, and we have the car," Peter told Dagmar. "The only
problem we'll have is how to bring it over to the U.S."

Dagmar was a bit more skeptical. "Maybe it will take longer. But a week or
two won't make a difference," she assured him.

They started their search on January 10, 2001, by writing a letter to the head of the German government, Chancellor Gerhard Schröder. They told him about the Paper Clip Project and asked for his help in locating a railcar. He sent a courteous reply but said he was unable to help.

They wrote to the president of the German rail company. During the war, this company, the Deutsche Reichsbahn, had transported prisoners to the concentration camps. Everyone at the company knew what was happening. Workers often wore earplugs to block out the screams of the frightened, the sick, and the dying. The Reichsbahn had made a lot of money on their cargo of death.

"What the kids in Whitwell are doing is very interesting," a company official answered, "and I wish them good luck. But unfortunately there are no *Güterwagen* (boxcars) left from that time."

They wrote more letters and made more phone calls: to railroad museums, to private rail companies, and to rail experts all over Europe. Some resented being asked. "Another Holocaust memorial? It's time to forget what happened 60 years ago." But most replied with the simple message: no railcar.

The Schroeders knew there were many people of goodwill in Germany: people who had written and sent paper clips, people who, after the horrors of the Holocaust, wanted to speak out against intolerance, hate, and racism.

In April, Dagmar called her travel agent. "We want to go to Munich—tomorrow," she announced. The next afternoon, the Schroeders flew from Washington, D.C., to Munich, Germany, rented a car, and started their journey—through Germany and neighboring Austria, Belgium, and the Netherlands. They hunted through old rail yards, but nothing was suitable

for the Holocaust memorial. They knew all the cars they found had been built after World War II because the boxcars the Nazis used had two fixed axles and four wheels. Cars introduced after the war had two tandem axles and eight wheels.

They drove more than 2,000 miles through Europe without success. They returned to Munich planning to e-mail the children of Whitwell the unhappy news. But as they prepared to fly home to Washington, they received a phone call from Professor Klaus Hübotter, a good friend in Bremen, Germany.

"My son-in-law Reiner Schümer has found what you are looking for," Hübotter said. "There is a small railroad museum north of Berlin that owns a cattle car from the time of Nazis. Go and get it!"

But the railcar was not for sale.

TRAIN STATION AT GANZLIN, GERMANY, HOME OF THE RAILROAD MUSEUM

CHAPTER SIX

THE CAR IS FOUND

CAR NUMBER 011–993
AT THE GERMAN
RAILROAD MUSEUM

THE DIRECTOR of the railroad museum had bad news. "Yes, we have a cattle car from the Nazi era," he told the Schroeders. "It has quite a history. You can come to look at it. But it is not for sale."

An hour later, they began the 500-mile drive to meet with the museum director who was also a manager at the headquarters of the German Rail Company in Berlin. Dagmar was convinced that when he heard the story of the Paper Clip Project face-to-face, he would change his mind.

The museum was 60 miles away, but the director, Dr. Rainer Zache, offered to drive with them to see the car. "Our museum is called Eisenbahnverein Ganzlin e.V. Röbel,*" he told them. "You know we Germans love long and complicated names."

When they first saw the long row of old freight cars, they were disappointed. Most had been built after World War II, and some were not even German. Other cars from the time of the Nazis had been remodeled into sleeping quarters for rail workers, complete with windows, kitchens, and stairways.

But then they saw it, and it took their breath away: Car Number 011–993, built in 1917. It looked like all the other cars that were used for KZL-Transporte (transports to concentration camps). The Schroeders had studied old pictures over and over again, "and we knew that we had found our car."

The museum staff had researched the history of Car Number 011–993. There were indications that the car had been abandoned in 1945 at the Polish town of Sobibor. Nearby was one of the major Nazi extermination camps. Most probably, the car had been used to transport Jews and others to the hands of their murderers.

"The precise history of this railcar will never be known," Dagmar said. "But I know one thing for sure: whatever its history was, it is over. Its future will be different."

"Please help us," they asked the museum director. "The students in Whitwell are collecting eleven million paper clips, one for each victim of the Nazis. The paper clips are symbols of people's lives. They should be preserved in one of the railcars that brought them to their deaths."

* Railroad Club Ganzlin/Röbel (the two neighboring towns where the museum is located).

"I really would like to help you," the director said, "but my hands are tied. We searched long and hard to get a railcar like this, and without it our collection would be incomplete."

The Schroeders feared that they had come to another dead end. What would they tell the students at Whitwell?

Dagmar had a final question for the head of the railroad museum. "Do you have children, Herr Direktor?" she asked him.

"Yes," he answered. "I have a young daughter, and I love her very much."

Dagmar persisted. "One and a half million children were killed during the Holocaust, children like your daughter, Herr Direktor. Many of them were transported to their deaths in cattle cars like this one. One and a half million of the paper clips in Whitwell are the symbols of their lives. The Holocaust memorial will be a constant reminder that we all have to strive to make sure that this history is not repeated."

At first, the director said nothing. Then he smiled. "I understand. We will sell you the railcar for the same price we paid for it."

"We found it!" the e-mail to Whitwell said. "The railcar is coming."

THE COMMUNITY PITCHES IN

CHAPTER SEVEN

PREPARING THE GROUND TO INSTALL THE RAILROAD TRACKS IN FRONT OF THE SCHOOL

THE NEWS that the Schroeders had found a railcar triggered a flurry of activity back in Tennessee. Linda Hooper organized a town meeting, and people came in droves. Kids rode their bicycles and skateboards, adults walked or drove, and young couples pushed their baby strollers. Some wore work clothes, others their Sunday best. The mayor and the police chief came. So did the members of the local senior citizens club.

"The students of this school will build a Holocaust memorial," the principal told the audience, "and we need your help. We are getting a railcar from Germany that was used to transport prisoners to concentration camps. This

33

historic car will be the focal point of our memorial and will house eleven million paper clips as symbols of the lives lost."

"Lord have mercy!" a man in the audience exclaimed. "Building a Holocaust memorial is something for big city folks."

Linda answered. "I'm not sure I have the slightest idea how to build a memorial either, but I do know one thing: If we all work together, we can do it. We can build a memorial that will show the world that we care." People in the audience applauded.

"Here's what we need," she continued. "We need carpenters and electricians. We need people for landscaping. Gosh, we need people for everything. Sign up, folks. Leave your names, addresses, and phone numbers. We will call you as soon we need your helping hands." Everyone signed up.

COMMUNITY MEMBERS PLANT SHRUBS AT THE MEMORIAL SITE.

Principal Hooper also reported that an independent film company had requested permission to come down to Whitwell to film a documentary. All agreed that the Paper Clip Project was important and that, if more people knew about it, they could learn from it.

They knew that lives had already been changed by the project. "There was one girl in our Holocaust class that we didn't like very much," a student admitted. "She didn't do anything to us, but we teased her a lot, and she was pretty lonely. You might say she was an outcast. But she didn't complain.

"One day, Ms. Roberts explained how the Nazis began their anti-Semitic campaign. For no reason, people were told not to like Jews anymore, so they stopped greeting their Jewish neighbors even if they had been friends for years. And when the police came and took the Jews away, neighbors looked the other way and didn't do anything.

"I told myself that it could not happen in our community. Then I thought about the girl in our class," the student went on. "She hasn't done anything to us, and still we treat her like she doesn't exist. What would we do if the police came for her? Look the other way?

"Then I realized that what we were doing was not very different from what a lot of Germans did. In Germany, 'not caring' made the Holocaust possible, and we had to care about our fellow students."

CHAPTER EIGHT

THE JOURNEY BEGINS

**INSTALLING ONE OF THE
SIGNS ON THE RAILCAR**

WITH FINANCIAL HELP from family and friends, the Schroeders were able to purchase the railcar. Now the problem was to transport it more than 5,000 miles—from the rail museum in Germany over the Atlantic Ocean to Whitwell. The only way was by sea. But the nearest seaport was 300 miles away from the museum.

It was time to call the German rail company again. This time they were eager to help. "Of course we can move the railcar, but it will be expensive," the representative said.

"How expensive?" Peter asked.

"I'm no expert," the woman said, "but you are looking at a bill of at least $10,000."

"It's for a Holocaust memorial," the Schroeders reminded her. "Can't you do it a little bit cheaper?"

"How cheap?" they were asked.

"How about for free?" Dagmar suggested. "The company can donate their services as a gesture of goodwill."

At first, the woman at the rail company said nothing. But after a while, she said in a low voice, "You are definitely right. We should help the kids build their Holocaust memorial. It is time for a German rail company to demonstrate that it cares."

She promised to talk to her boss. "Give me two or three days to work this thing out," she said. But she called back the next day. "We will do it. For free. Tell us where to send it."

There were still several problems to solve. The railcar could not be transported on a flatbed car, as it would exceed height restrictions. Most of the tracks in Germany are electrified, and a railcar on a flatbed would hit the overhead cables. It would be difficult to find stretches of track without cables. So the railroad officials sent a team of experts to the museum to look at the car to see if it could roll on its own wheels.

The Schroeders waited for the engineers' verdict at their daughter's house in

THE RAILCAR ROLLS THROUGH THE GERMAN COUNTRYSIDE ON ITS OWN WHEELS.

northern Germany. They decided that the railcar should be dressed up for its arrival in the United States. It was no longer an ordinary railcar—it was part of a memorial. "The memorial needs signs," their son-in-law Martin suggested, "and we have two friends who are sign makers."

"But what shall the sign say?" their daughter Silke asked. "You need to call it something special."

"Of course it will be something special," the Schroeders answered. Then switching to English, they said, "It will be The Children's Holocaust Memorial."

Their five-year-old granddaughter Anna-Lea repeated the unfamiliar English words again and again: "The Children's Holocaust Memorial."

The adults laughed, and everyone knew that it was an appropriate name, because the memorial was being created by children for children.

They decided to create two signs to put on the car before it started its journey through Germany: "The Children's Holocaust Memorial" would be on one side and a sign with the German translation, "Holocaust-Mahnmal der Kinder," on the other. The two sign makers, Wolfgang, a German, and Hans from the neighboring Netherlands, worked through the night. "These are the most important signs we ever made," they told the Schroeders.

The next problem that had to be solved was how to get the railcar over the Atlantic. The Schroeders knew that the German military shipped equipment back and forth to the United States. So they called Jürgen Chrobog, an old friend from Washington, who was now undersecretary of the German Foreign Ministry.

THE SCHROEDERS, THEIR GRANDDAUGHTERS, AND A GOOD FRIEND AT THE SEND-OFF CEREMONY FOR THE RAILCAR

He, in turn, spoke to an undersecretary in the German Ministry of Defense, who, in turn, approached his boss. "O.K.," was the response. "We will put The Children's Holocaust Memorial railcar on the next transport ship to the United States."

By that time, the woman from the rail company had called with good news: "Our technician fixed the car so it can roll on its own wheels," she reported. "We can start the journey the day after tomorrow. But we will have to go slowly, no faster than 30 miles per hour."

Since every train in Germany has to have an official name, this train would be called Special Train-Holocaust Memorial. On August 23, 2001, the railcar was hooked to a heavy locomotive. An additional brake car was attached, because the experts didn't trust the air brakes on the memorial car. After a send-off ceremony that was covered by TV, radio, and newspaper reporters, the Special Train-Holocaust Memorial began its 300-mile long journey through Germany.

The train had to stop every 30 miles to grease the axles and the wheels and to let faster trains go by. After a full day and night, the train arrived in the German port of Cuxhaven on the North Sea.

Here a new problem arose. There is a wood-eating bug in Europe that is unknown in the United States. To prevent the importation of this bug, any wood product entering the country has to be disinfected. The U.S. Department of Agriculture told the Schroeders that the railcar had to be dipped in a chemical bath. But where could one find a bathtub big enough for a railcar? Another solution was found. A high-powered water gun was used to spray the chemicals onto the car.

The railcar was ready for its transatlantic voyage.

HOLOCAUST SURVIVORS VISIT WHITWELL.

CHAPTER NINE

THE SURVIVORS VISIT WHITWELL

BACK IN WHITWELL, the Holocaust took on a human face, actually four faces. Holocaust survivors from New York learned about the Whitwell Paper Clip Project and asked Linda Hooper if they could visit. They wanted to meet the students and thank them.

Before a packed audience of students, parents, teachers, and other members of the community, the four visitors, all in their seventies and eighties, shared stories of their lives in the camps. "We were the lucky ones," one man said. "We made it out alive and are able to tell the story."

The students were stunned. They had read about the Holocaust, they had discussed the fate of the victims, but they had never met people who had actually been there. Tears flowed and people hugged, as the film crew recorded the meeting for its documentary.

One survivor said, "I can't believe the outpouring of love from these children. They are embracing strangers, and they are fighting against evil. The world is a better place because of them."

As the survivors bade farewell to the "good people of Whitwell," a freighter steamed into the German port of Cuxhaven.

CHAPTER TEN

CROSSING THE ATLANTIC

WHEN THE SCHROEDERS saw the ship *Blue Sky*, they looked at each other in disbelief. The ship's home port was Bergen. "This is a Norwegian ship!" Peter exclaimed. People in Norway had started the paper clip movement to protest the treatment of Jews. The Norwegian postal service had recently issued a stamp to honor Johan Vaaler, the inventor of the paper clip. And now, a Norwegian ship would transport the railcar destined for The Children's Holocaust Memorial of the Paper Clip Project.

The harbormaster ordered all other work in the harbor to stop while the memorial was loaded onto the ship. As the railcar rolled onto *Blue Sky*,

THE RAILCAR ON BOARD *BLUE SKY*

the longshoremen removed their hats and military personnel saluted. The last person to board was a high-ranking German army officer whose sole responsibility was to watch over the car.

Two hours later, *Blue Sky* headed out to the open sea. The following night, it cleared the English Channel and steamed toward the U.S. coast. The sea was calm. The 4,000-mile journey to the port of Baltimore was expected to take approximately 13 days. The captain told the Schroeders not to worry. In case of a storm, he would slow down the ship to minimize rolling. "We will take good care of the memorial," he assured them. "This trip will be a piece of cake."

But it was not to be. "A storm front is approaching very fast," the radio operator told the ship's captain.

The skipper looked at his charts. "Can we avoid it?"

"Not a chance. It's a very broad front. Wherever we turn, the storm will hit us and it will hit us hard," the radio operator answered.

It was not yet noon, but the sky was already dark. The captain called the bridge. "Slow speed ahead. We will hit waves up to 30 feet. I will come up when it gets rough." He instructed the crew to remove every item from the hold that could fly or roll. They checked every chain and made sure that the military cargo could not break free and get tossed around. A rolling tank could puncture the vessel's hull and cause the ship to sink.

For more than six hours, the captain stayed at the wheel and "rode the waves." Frantically, he steered the vessel head on, as big walls of water slammed the deck. *Blue Sky* shuddered, but she stayed afloat. Then, as quickly as the storm came, it went. The sea was calm again, and everyone relaxed.

A short time later, the sailors heard a noise they all dreaded. It was the noise of no noise at all. The engine had stopped. "The main oil pump blew," the machine room called to the captain. "We are trying to repair it."

All day the engineers worked tirelessly. *Blue Sky* was dead in the water. Without the engine running, nobody could steer the vessel, and the wind was blowing it off course. Thankfully, the radio was still usable. The captain called the U.S. Coast Guard to inform them that the ship was drifting and to warn off other vessels in the vicinity. After 14 hours of silence, the engine of *Blue Sky* came back to life. In roughly 20 more hours, the ship would dock in Baltimore, Maryland.

But the 20 hours became two days. Once in U.S. territorial waters, the Coast Guard ordered the captain to stop for an inspection. Every vessel that enters a U.S. port has to have a Coast Guard certificate. *Blue Sky* didn't have one, because it had never sailed to the United States. The officers boarded and found everything in order. When they saw the railcar, the joking and the lighthearted comments stopped. The officers touched the sign that read "The Children's Holocaust Memorial." No one tried to open the doors or even to peer inside.

Blue Sky arrived at the Baltimore harbor on September 9, 2001. The railcar was off-loaded first and put on a flatbed car from the American rail company CSX, which

THE RAILCAR IS OFF-LOADED TO A CSX TRAIN IN BALTIMORE.

had offered its services to Whitwell, free of charge. Two days later, the flatbed car was attached to a big diesel locomotive and began the final leg of its journey. The date was September 11, 2001.

As the memorial, a symbol of tolerance, rolled slowly through the countryside, terrorists struck the United States. They slammed passenger planes into the World Trade Center in New York City and the Pentagon in Washington, D.C. Another hijacked plane crashed in Pennsylvania. Nearly 3,000 people lost their lives.

The students of Whitwell Middle School mourned with the rest of the world. For three years, they had worked to fight hate and intolerance. They watched the tragedy on TV with tears in their eyes. Nobody could talk. Finally, one girl spoke up.

"If I had not known why we are building a memorial," she said, "I would know it now."

CHAPTER ELEVEN

THE RAILCAR COMES HOME

**THE RAILCAR MAKES
ITS WAY TO WHITWELL.**

As THE RAILCAR rolled toward Tennessee, the people of Whitwell were busy preparing for its arrival. Workers from the rail company CSX had arrived with trucks and a bulldozer. They cleared a patch of lawn in front of the school to lay down railway tracks for the German car.

The workers had searched for the oldest tracks they could find, and they had brought tracks manufactured in 1947, the year many Jews liberated from Nazi concentration camps had immigrated to America.

The day the railcar arrived in Whitwell, life in the town came to a standstill.

People skipped work, businesses and shops closed, and everyone gathered at the school to wait.

In Chattanooga the railcar had been transferred to a big truck for the slow drive over the mountains to the Sequatchie Valley. As the truck approached Whitwell, police cars with flashing lights cleared the way through town, up a little hill to Main Street, and finally to the school.

A big crane lifted the railcar from the truck and carefully put it down on the tracks. When the iron wheels touched the iron tracks, they made no sound. But the more than 400 students of Whitwell Middle School cheered. They jumped up and down in joy, while the adults clapped in appreciation. Then the students, their parents, grandparents, neighbors, and teachers quietly approached the car and touched it. Many people cried.

Car Number 011–993 had reached its final destination. A railcar that had

THE RAILCAR ON MAIN STREET NEARING THE SCHOOL

witnessed so much misery was now a testament to what people of goodwill could accomplish, and it was proof that kids can achieve almost anything if they are determined.

The next day, Kevin Higdon, a local contractor, took charge. "Normally we build houses," he told David Smith, "but the memorial will be a house too, a house of symbols."

A lumber company donated material, and Kevin, his father Herbert, his wife Mary Jane, and a crew went to work. They repaired the railcar's old roof and gave it a new floor. They built wooden stairs and a ramp for visitors in wheelchairs or with strollers.

In the meantime, the students from the Holocaust class were busy designing the interior of the memorial. They decided to put 11 million paper clips into

BUILDING STAIRS TO THE RAILCAR

ERECTING THE SECOND MEMORIAL TO HOLD AN ADDITIONAL 11 MILLION PAPER CLIPS

the railcar—6 million for the Jewish victims and 5 million for all the others. The paper clips would be visible behind two glass partitions on either side of the car.

"Finally we will be able to see what millions look like," the kids said. "We started the whole project because we wanted to see, to feel, and to touch such a big number and to try to understand what the Nazis had done."

The students had calculated that 30 paper clips weighed roughly one ounce. The 11 million paper clips would weigh about 11 metric tons. Several heavy trucks would be needed to transport them to the memorial.

At the beginning of November, the students began filling the memorial. The paper clips that had been collected one by one were trucked to the memorial site, hauled up the ramp in wheelbarrows, and carefully placed behind the glass partitions.

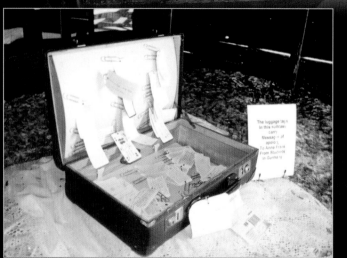

(*TOP*) PETER SCHROEDER PLACES THE LAST
PAPER CLIPS BEHIND GLASS INSIDE THE
RAILCAR.   (*LEFT*) AMONG THE ARTIFACTS ON
DISPLAY IN THE RAILCAR IS A SUITCASE FROM
THE 1940S SENT FROM A CLASS IN GERMANY.
IT IS FILLED WITH NOTES TO ANNE FRANK,
ASKING HER FOR FORGIVENESS.

When the last of the 11 million were behind glass, the students could only stare. They had wanted to see millions of something to get a feel for the sheer size of the Holocaust. They had succeeded, and they were overwhelmed.

One boy had put 1,600 paper clips aside in a shoebox. "We have 1,600 people in Whitwell," he told Sandra Roberts. "If we had been victims of the Nazis, if they had killed every living soul in Whitwell, and if some kids somewhere else had started a paper clip project, these paper clips would represent us."

Over the next few days, some yards in Whitwell were noticeably emptier than they had been before. Their owners had dug up plants and flowers and had brought them to the school. "It should look nice around here," members of the landscaping committee told Linda Hooper. And within a week, the memorial stood in the middle of a blossoming garden.

Isabel Condra, the 84-year-old unofficial town historian, documented the progress in her weekly column for the *Jasper Journal,* the local paper. In one of her columns, she wondered, "Is there a living soul in Whitwell who has not helped with the project? I don't think so."

Linda Pickett, a gifted artist and owner of the flower shop near the school, was busy too. She poured concrete into the shape of butterflies and painted them. They would be embedded in the walkway up to the railcar. Pickett had read a poem by Pavel Friedmann, a child imprisoned in the ghetto of Terezin.

"Only I never saw a butterfly. That butterfly was the last one," he wrote. "Butterflies don't live in here, in the ghetto."*

* From "The Butterfly" by Pavel Friedmann, in . . . *I Never Saw Another Butterfly: Children's Drawings and Poems from Terezin Concentration Camp 1942–1944,* ed. Hana Volavkova. (Prague: Artia, 1978; New York: Schocken Books, Inc., 1993.)

CHAPTER TWELVE

DEDICATING THE MEMORIAL

SCHOOL MARQUEE ANNOUNCING THE

DEDICATION OF THE MEMORIAL

NOVEMBER 9, 2001, was a perfect day for butterflies in Whitwell, Tennessee. It was a warm day with bright sunshine. It was a weekday, but nobody had to attend classes. The Children's Holocaust Memorial was to be officially dedicated. It was the sixty-third anniversary of Kristallnacht, the Night of Broken Glass—the date in 1938 when the Nazis torched synagogues, looted Jewish-owned businesses, and committed murder.

In this town of 1,600 citizens, close to 2,000 people attended the dedication. The Schroeders were there, along with their son Bjørn from London. They brought small stones that their grandchildren Pia, Jule, and Anna-Lea had

(ABOVE) **STUDENTS AND COMMUNITY LEADERS GATHER FOR THE DEDICATION.** (RIGHT) **THE UNIVERSITY OF CHATTANOOGA ORCHESTRA AT THE DEDICATION**

collected at the rail tracks in the little town in Germany where they live. Following Jewish tradition, stones, not flowers, are placed at gravesites to remember the dead.

School and community representatives spoke, the orchestra of the University in Chattanooga played, the school choir sang, and prayers were offered by members of different religious denominations. Students from an Atlanta Jewish Day School recited Kaddish, the Jewish prayer for the dead.

However, what the students wanted most was for everyone to see what they had built, a symbolic resting place for millions of victims who have no graves.

As the guests at the dedication walked silently through the memorial, one student took Sandra Roberts's hand. "We showed the world that there is another way than hate and intolerance, didn't we?" she told her teacher.

CHAPTER THIRTEEN

THE PROJECT CONTINUES

INSIDE THE RAILCAR

SINCE THE DEDICATION, schools from all over the country are contacting the Holocaust group in Whitwell. Many had sent paper clips for the memorial, and now they want to start Holocaust projects of their own.

The students are encouraging these schools. "We received close to thirty million paper clips," the Whitwell students explain. "As you know, eleven million are now in our memorial in the railcar for all who were murdered by the Nazis. And we put eleven million more into another monument next to the railcar. It is a sealed steel container, and it will house the paper clips forever. Nobody will be able to touch these paper clips again. They will be safe. But we have eight million paper clips remaining at the school, and we are happy to make them available to other schools who submit project proposals."

The students have outlined the kinds of projects others could undertake. For example, a class could do research about a town in Europe during the war. "Find out how many Jews lived there when the Nazis took over and how many survived," they suggest. "Then you can figure out how many victims in this town were murdered. Tell us what you find out, and we will send you that number of paper clips." Currently, many schools in the United States, Canada, Germany, Austria, and Italy are doing projects like these.

And school classes from all over the country are making field trips to The Children's Holocaust Memorial. The visiting students hear lectures about the Holocaust and the Paper Clip Project. But it's not the teachers who are lecturing, it's the students.

And the lecture begins, "When we started this project we didn't know anything about the Holocaust. But then we learned that millions of people were murdered just because other people didn't like them. During the Holocaust, the Nazis murdered six million Jews."

Then the student guides ask a question: "Do you know how many six million is?"

Nobody knows.

So the students invite everybody to follow. "Come with us; we will show you."

Then they all go to the railcar and see.

MEMBERS OF THE HOLOCAUST GROUP OF WHITWELL MIDDLE SCHOOL

SCHOOL YEAR 1998–1999

Miranda Ables

Sherrill Atterton

Candice Boston

Angie Castle

Coby Curvin

Laura Davis

Jessica Giles

Tyler Hancock

Ashley McGowan

Ashley Lofty

Christy Nunley

Jessica Partin

Jarvis Powell

Lindsey Rollins

Nicole Sanders

Jennifer Vandergriff

SCHOOL YEAR 1999–2000

Chad Ables

Steven Austin

Molly Bailey

Chris Brown

Mindy Bryant

Amanda Elliott

Eric Fine

Felicia Floyd

David Flynn

Monica Hammers

Jonathan Higdon

Ashley Hooks

Breeze Hudson

Chris Johnson

Bruce Kilgore

Laurie Lynn

Holly Norman

Holly Perkins

CHRIS PRIVETT

ROBBYN REYNOLDS

JESSICA SHIPLEY

JAIDE TERRY

LANCE WEBB

SCHOOL YEAR 2000–2001

JORDAN CARROLL

ASHLEY CLEMONS

CASEY CONDRA

HEATH COOKSTONE

TALENA COOKSTONE

CASSIE CRABTREE

CHADDI HATFIELD

ELIZABETH HENRY

CASSIE HIGGINS

LAURA JEFFRIES

MITCH KILGORE

DAVID KING

TAYLOR LAWSON

MYLES PARRIS

TORY RAULSTON

TASHAWNNA SEBER

DREW SHADRICK

ROBYN SISCO

ALLISON THOMAS

LATOSHA WORLEY

SCHOOL YEAR 2001–2002

TREY BELL

JOSEPH BAILEY

KRISTIN CLEMONS

JAYA COOKSTONE

RYAN COOKSTONE

TERRI LYNN FLOYD

WENDY FLOYD

CHRIS FOX

ALLISON HALL

AMANDA HEADRICK

CARIE KILGORE

KATIE LAYNE

Thomas Martin

Ashley Miller

Judy Morrison

Jeremy Nunley

Randi Perkey

Meagan Powell

Brittany Reynolds

Jessica Reynolds

Jessi Royer

Greg Stalyon

Ryan Thomas

Tavis Tripp

Kyle Upchurch

Jessica Vandergriff

Tiffany Whittemore

SCHOOL YEAR 2002–2003

Shanna Atterton

Callie Bird

Leanne Carr

Ronny Carr

Kayla Cates

Carrie Davidson

Lacey Essex

Brandi Grayson

Lindsey Hamblin

Daniel Hooks

Amanda Hooper

Daniel King

Tiffany Matherly

Ashley A. Morrison

Ashley R. Morrison

Hannah Mosier

Lorie Nelson

Jessica Nunley

Kellie Nunley

Amber Powell

Kristan Pyburn

Christal Sanders

Emily Sanders

Felicia Scissom

Colton Shadrick

Latasha Shirley

Whitney Terry

Carrie Thomas

Jessica Vandergriff

April White

SCHOOL YEAR 2003–2004

SHEA ABLES

JERRICA AKINS

JESSICA ATTERTON

BRITTANY BARNETT

SHANDA BARNETT

DANIELLE BRYANT

KENDI CAGLE

DUSTIN CHANCE

NATASHA CRAWLEY

MEGAN DEFUR

WHITNEY DODSON

JENNY FRAZIER

HEATHER FULFER

HEATHER GOFORTH

KAITI HUBBARD

BRITTANY HUCKABY

TIFFANY JONES

MAKENZIE KETCHERSID

AMANDA KILGORE

CASSY KILGORE

KAYLA LAYNE

AARON LONG

KRISTEN LONG

CELESTE MCCOY

BRITTANY MCGOWAN

ELEUTERIO MARES

JULIA MORRISON

LINDSEY NIPPER

BRANDI NUNLEY

ANNA PICKETT

CASSIE POWELL

PAIGE RIDGE

LEAH SHRUM

SHEA THOMAS

TISH THOMAS

HALEY VANDAGRIFF

AMBER WEBB

CHAD WHIDBY

ALEX WHITTEMORE

CANDACE WOODS

JOSH WOODWARD

STEPHEN YOUNG

NEVER DOUBT THAT A GROUP OF THOUGHTFUL, COMMITED STUDENTS CAN CHANGE THE WORLD— ONE CLASS AT A TIME.

–FROM THE CHILDREN'S HOLOCAUST MEMORIAL SIGN

ONE OF THE CONCRETE BUTTERFLIES LINING THE PATH TO THE MEMORIAL

ABOUT THE TEACHERS

"I became a teacher because my parents placed great emphasis on education and the importance of giving back to the community. Next to family and friends, The Children's Holocaust Memorial is the most important thing in my life."

SANDRA ROBERTS, codirector of the Holocaust group, is an eighth-grade teacher and the cheerleading coach at Whitwell, the school she attended herself. Sandra is single but claims to have "425 kids—all the students at the school." Sandra has taught all of the Holocaust classes.

"It is our duty as teachers to educate our students about the evil of hatred, bigotry, racism, and intolerance. And we must show our students that they can make a difference in this ever-changing world."

DAVID ALAN SMITH, vice principal of Whitwell Middle School and codirector of the Holocaust Group, has been teaching for 11 years. He serves also as athletic director and head coach for the school's football, baseball, and track teams. David and his wife, Laura, have two sons, Cody and Devin.

"The Paper Clip Project has been an affirmation of my beliefs that education is absolutely essential to change; everyone must study the past so that we do not forget or repeat our mistakes."

LINDA M. HOOPER has been the principal of Whitwell Middle School for 10 years and a public school teacher for 30 years. She and Edward, her husband of 41 years, have two children and four grandchildren. Linda enjoys reading, traveling, furniture refinishing, painting, and hiking.

ABOUT THE AUTHORS

PETER W. SCHROEDER, born in 1942 in Germany, is an economist. He worked as a diplomatic correspondent in Europe, Asia, Israel, and for the last 24 years in North America. His books deal mostly with German history, tolerance, the Holocaust, and European-American relations. He and his wife live in Washington, D.C.; Victoria, Canada; and a little town in Germany.

DAGMAR SCHROEDER-HILDEBRAND, born in 1943 in Germany, is a psychologist. She was editor in chief of a magazine for parents of handicapped children. She also worked as a diplomatic correspondent in different parts of the world. She is the author of several biographies of Holocaust survivors.

INDEX

PHOTO AND REPRODUCTION ACKNOWLEDGMENTS

The images in this book are used with the permission of:
© Bjørn Ole Schroeder, cover and pp. 6, 63 (bottom two)
© Todd Strand/Independent Picture Service, back cover and pp. 1, 2
© Dagmar and Peter Schroeder, pp. 4, 5, 7, 8, 11 (both), 13, 15, 18 (both), 21 (both), 23, 24, 25,
27, 29, 30, 36, 38, 39, 43, 44, 46 (both), 52 (top), 54, 55 (both), 56, 58, 61, 63 (bottom)
© Mary Jane and Kevin Higdon, pp. 16, 17, 33, 34, 41, 48, 49, 50, 51, 52 (bottom), 58, 60
© Ulrich Störiko-Blume, p. 20
Courtesy of Sandra Roberts, pp. 59, 62 (top)
Courtesy of David Smith, p. 62 (bottom)
Courtesy of Linda Hooper, p. 63 (top)